IMAGES OF WAR

Liberators in England during World War II

RARE PHOTOGRAPHS FROM WARTIME ARCHIVES

PETER W. BODLE FRAeS

Pen & Sword
AVIATION

First published in Great Britain in 2008 by
PEN & SWORD AVIATION
An imprint of
Pen & Sword Books Ltd
47 Church Street
Barnsley
South Yorkshire
S70 2AS

Copyright © Peter Bodle, 2008

ISBN 978 1 84415 821 8

The right of Peter Bodle to be identified as Author of this work
has been asserted by him in accordance with the
Copyright, Designs and Patents Act 1988.

A CIP catalogue record for this book is
available from the British Library

Typeset by Phoenix Typesetting, Auldgirth, Dumfriesshire
Printed and bound in Great Britain by CPI UK

Pen & Sword Books Ltd incorporates the Imprints of
Pen & Sword Aviation, Pen & Sword Family History, Pen & Sword Maritime,
Pen & Sword Military, Wharncliffe Local History, Pen & Sword Select,
Pen & Sword Military Classics, Leo Cooper, Remember When, Seaforth Publishing
and Frontline Publishing

For a complete list of Pen & Sword titles please contact
PEN & SWORD BOOKS LIMITED
47 Church Street, Barnsley, South Yorkshire, S70 2AS, England
E-mail: enquiries@pen-and-sword.co.uk
Website: www.pen-and-sword.co.uk

Contents

Introduction

The Consolidated Liberator, the B-24, was produced in greater quantities than any other American aircraft during the years of WWII (18,000+), and probably served in more roles than any aircraft on either side of the conflict. They cost $215,516.00 per aircraft to build. ($1.00 was worth just 50p at the exchange rate of the day)

Over the years, the B-24 was powered by various variants of the two row, 14 Cylinder, 30 Litre, Air-Cooled, Pratt and Whitney R 1830 radial piston engine. It was almost certainly the most widely produced aero engine on the allies' side of the conflict with 173,618 units being built.

It is well documented that the RAF received a few B-24s in the early part of the war, following the collapse of France, and then took over the remainder of the order for 139 aircraft, originally placed by the French Government. It was not however until 1942 that this huge aircraft started to become a daily sight over the flat lands of East Anglia as the USAAF 8th Air Force established itself on English soil and began contributing to the war effort on a regular basis. By then many of the RAF's Liberators were operating overseas.

The 2nd Air Division (2nd AD), formerly referred to as the 2nd Bombardment Division, was the division of the Mighty Eighth Air Force of the USAAF. (Previously named the USAAC, United States Army Air Corps) that was designated to take on the Liberator and operate it in the European Theatre of Operations (ETO). Based mainly, although not totally, in Norfolk, they were responsible for the greater majority of the Liberators seen in the sky over the South and East of England. The 2nd AD was made up of four Bomb Wings, the 2nd, 14th, 20th and 96th , plus the oddball and very short lived 95th, with each wing comprising of three or four Bomb Groups. Each of the main Bomb Groups occupied one airfield and generally had four Bomb Squadrons. They flew a total of 98,948 sorties and dropped almost 200,000 tons of bombs in the process.

A few other Squadrons operated Liberators from airfields inside Norfolk, and further afield, including some for experimental work, or other more 'discrete' purposes than bombing, but these were relatively few and far between.

The Bomb Wings were

2nd	HQ	Hethel	Hethel, Tibenham, Old Buckenham
14th	HQ	Shipdham	Shipdham, Wendling, North Pickenham
20th	HQ	Hardwick	Seething, Bungay(Flixton), Hardwick
95th	HQ	Halesworth	Halesworth, Metfield
96th	HQ	Horsham St Faith	Horsham St Faith, Attlebridge, Rackheath

(When the 95th Bomb Wing disbanded, the 491st Bomb Group at Metfield went to North Pickenham and joined the 14th Bomb Wing, and the 489th at Halesworth were integrated into the 20th Bomb Wing.)

Like so many aircraft built for warfare in that era, the B24 was constantly being updated and many variants saw active service from their temporary Norfolk homes. The most widely used model designations were the D, H and J types, with the L and M variants coming in towards the end of the war. Within these groupings there were also several detailed variations, depending on where the individual plane was built and other minor variations . . . i.e. which of the gun turrets was fitted, if a radome was fitted for Pathfinder duties . . . that sort of thing.

They came from five production plants in the USA; San Diego, California, (Consolidated Aircraft Corporation); Fort Worth, Texas, (Consolidated Aircraft Corporation {Convair}); Willow Run, Michigan, (Ford Motor Company); Tulsa, Oklahoma, (Douglas Aircraft Company); Dallas, Texas, (North American Aviation).

Mainly the Liberators were flown across the Atlantic by the crews that had trained on them in the States. Some used the northern route via Greenland and Iceland, others a more southerly route via the Azores and West Africa. Several planes were lost on the way, predominantly on the northern route. Frequently the reason for their loss was never ascertained. For the USAAF it was the beginning of the harsh reality of wartime military flying.

The 44th Bomb Group at Shipdham, the 389th at Hethel and the 93rd at Hardwick were the first Liberator equipped crews to arrive. They started to get to Norfolk in the late autumn of 1942 and immediately set to learning all about their new homes, their roles in the conflict raging just over the English Channel and their newly acquired English hosts. Many of the first few missions flown by the Liberator crews were diversionary raids, sent up to help confuse the German defences and their early radar systems.

By the spring of 1943, all that was over and the operational Bomb Groups of the 2nd Air Division were fully engaged in tackling the enemy head on, flying daylight bombing missions against the enemy's industrial heartland, leaving the bombers of the RAF to fly during the hours of darkness.

Although never in sufficient quantities for the needs of the High Command of the USAAF, they were now being joined on an almost daily basis by more planes and crews from the training squadrons in America. Their ground crews, in their thousands, and all the back-up equipment they would need to keep this ever growing fleet airborne, were also pouring across the Atlantic at a similar rate, aboard freighters, troop carriers and converted luxury liners.

Whilst every effort has been made to ensure the accuracy in this book, the author acknowledges that sixty three years on from the cessation of hostilities, some records are to say the least, vague or conflicting. It must also be pointed out that some aircraft names were used on several different aircraft, sometimes by the same bomb group, sometimes by several different groups.

This book, featuring photographs mainly provided from private archives, lovingly collected and preserved over the years by English archivists, is dedicated to every airman of the Mighty Eighth, who ever set foot aboard one of these magnificent aircraft in order to free the world of Nazi dictatorship and tyranny.

Acknowledgements

Almost all the photos in this book are from or via the Tony North collection. I am delighted to place on record my heartfelt thanks to Tony for allowing me access to this fabulous archive and for all the assistance and guidance given by him in the preparation of this book.

Grateful thanks are also due to some of the B-24's most enthusiastic and knowledgeable archivists and historians, who have also contributed in no small measure to my understanding of this aircraft and the accuracy of this book. They are Steve Adams, Mike Bailey, Alan Blue, Pat Everson, Brian Mahoney and Paul Wilson. Where aircraft names have been used several times by different Bomb Groups or where the name has been repeated in the same group several times and where numbers have been obliterated by either battle damage or wear and tear, this unrivalled, collective expertise has been invaluable.

My thanks go to my computer mentor, Mike Johnson, for his sterling efforts in de-aging many of the photos so that years of wear and tear, scratches, creases and marks are no longer visible on the photos in this book.

Finally to my wife Jane for providing all the patience and forbearance any writer's wife needs, in full measure, and indeed for all the long hours of initial proof reading put in to this and all my other works.

Peter W. Bodle. FRAeS
Stoke Ferry.

2nd Bombardment Wing

389th Bomb Group - Hethel

B-24 D, *The Little Gramper* (42-40722) from the 566th Bomb Squadron of the Hethel based 389th en-route to Germany early in the morning of Friday 24 November 1944.

Built at the Consolidated Aircraft Corporation's factory in San Diego, California, *The Little Gramper* survived this mission and many others and was eventually retired as War Weary, and later adapted for the role of assembly ship for the 491st Bomb Group at North Pickenham.

Missouri Mauler, a D model B-24 (42-63980) of the 567th Bomb Squadron photographed early in the conflict. It was built at the Consolidated Aircraft Corporation plant at Fort Worth, Texas. 980 was later transferred to the 801st Bomb Group at Harrington for clandestine operations with 'The Carpetbaggers', dropping agents and equipment into enemy held territory.

(42-63960), a D model built at the Consolidated Aircraft Corporation's Fort Worth, Texas, factory, seen here over a slightly choppy sea, en-route the Cognac district of France. 960 survived a dramatic forced landing in Kent on New Year's Eve '43, but was successfully repaired and returned to service.

Tuesday morning, high over Hanau on 12 Dec 1944, this B-24 of the 389th is about to unleash its bomb load to follow the smoke marker down into the railway marshalling yards thousands of feet below. Marshalling yards, road junctions, river crossings and other 'choke points' were favourite targets for the Bomb Groups of the 2nd Air Division.

This San Diego built B-24 J (42-100146) later became *Mistah Chick*, is seen here with its port waist gun aiming at something to the rear of the plane and elevated about 45 degrees. Initially it flew with the 564th then later with 567th Bomb Squadron. On the morning of Tuesday 20 June 1944 its luck ran out following a raid on Politz and it was forced to divert to Sweden, where its crew carried out a successful crash landing at Halmstad airfield, north of Helsingbourg.

One of the ground crews from the 567th Bomb Squadron give the No 2 engine on this B-24 D (42–40743) their full attention, during the spring of 1944. 743 already has amassed a mission tally of over fifty (including Ploesti), with more to come. 743 was a Consolidated Aircraft Corporation, San Diego built aircraft, from the early 1942 production run. The distinctive lines (yellow) on the bottom of the bomb doors were open/closed visual indicators. It later became the assembly ship for the 492nd Bomb Group.

One of the 546th Bomb Squadron's first Pathfinder aircraft (41-28784), looking decidedly well-worn as it tracks the Suffolk coast just inland from Southwold. 784 was ordered during 1941 from the Tulsa Oklahoma plant of The Douglas Aircraft Company, as part of Contract 18727. The Pathfinder radome is just visible between the port wing root and the fuselage.

For some, like the men of the runway maintenance teams, the rows of B-24s taxiing out to the runway threshold at Hethel, were almost impersonal. For others like the air crews and the engine fitters, these 1,200HP Pratt and Whitney radials were very much part of their everyday life. As were muddy wheels for the ground crews, when one of the taxiing aircraft missed the concrete. Digging them out of the Norfolk countryside on this and many other USAAF bases, was a fairly common occurrence in the winter or after heavy rain.

It was not only the USAAF who took pictures of the B-24. Here a German photographer has recorded the remains of (42-50617) as it lays a smouldering wreck in a field near Aschersleben, close to the foothills of the Harz Mountains, following the Mission to Halle on 7 July 1944. 617 was a Ford Motor Company built, J model, out of the Willow Run plant, flown by the 567th Squadron. It was one of five B-24s from the 389th Bomb Group lost on that same mission. (42-95029), (42-51144), (42-50374) and (41-28824) were also posted as MIA by the end of that fateful Friday afternoon. The pools of molten aluminium, now cooled and solidified under the wreckage, are a testament to the intensity of the post crash fire.

B-24 H (41-28779) of the 389th Bomb group was lost on one of the two missions flown by the 389th on Tuesday 20 June 1944. It was subsequently recovered by the Luftwaffe and flown under the swastika by Kampfgeschwader 200 (KG 200) for a while, before this incident which destroyed it.

Conquest Cavalier was a B-24 H from the 701st Bomb Squadron based at Tibenham (13 miles SSW of Norwich), with the 445th Bomb Group. Seen here above the clouds, (41-29126) was from the last batch of the H model to be built at Consolidated's Fort Worth plant in Texas. It was later transferred to the 446th Bomb Group at Bungay (Flixton).

This B-24 H (42-95308) of the 702nd Bomb Squadron, had its hydraulics damaged during a mission to bomb the synthetic oil refinery at Merseburg on Sunday 28 May 1944.

Parachutes were attached to fixing points in the interior of the fuselage and just before touchdown were deployed by the crew through the waist windows to provide braking for the aircraft.

The 701st Bomb Squadron's *Tahelenbak,* a B-24 H, (42-94921) with other 445th B-24s in the background. 921 was one of the last batch of H models produced to Contract 21216, at the Ford Motor Company's Willow Run plant. 921 also flew with the 703rd Bomb Squadron.

Lonesome Lois, (42-95020) a B-24 H from the 701st Bomb Squadron showing all the signs of the classic Consolidated Liberator front oleo collapse, having being diverted into Beccles, 14 July 1944. However the nose high attitude of *Blasted Event* (41-29487), another H variant from the 700th Bomb Squadron, is a really unusual scenario, presumably brought about by an incorrect weight and balance situation following a mission to re-supply Allied ground troops on Monday 18 Sept 1944.

A selection of very typical nose art from the 445th Bomb Group.

Able Mabel was a well used figure for USAAF nose art . . . this was the 445th version.

Sweetest Rose of Texas was B-24 H (42 – 76137) from 701st Bomb Squadron.

A neat play on words for the B-24 H, *Will - er - Run?* of the 702nd Bomb Squadron. Needless to say (42-7526) was built by Ford at the Willow Run Factory.

Q for Queenie had both an impressive 'mascot' as well as a hard earned tally of mission indicators. In April '44 it was damaged beyond repair and scrapped.

This B-24 J (42-100353) of the 703rd Bomb Squadron, was constructed at the Consolidated Plant in San Diego California and ended its last flight in a field at Fressingfield, close to Metfield Aerodrome in Suffolk on Wednesday 8 March 1944. Whilst when production of the B-24 was at its height, a new plane was rolling off the combined production lines every hour, it only took fractions of a second to reduce it to scrap. A wheels-down landing, even on rough ground, was always a preferred option.

Lillian Ann II (42-7571) at the end of its active service having slid off the runway at Dubendorf in Switzerland on Tuesday 11 July 1944. Damaged by flak during a raid on Munich, its Pilot, 1st Lt. Robert Gallup, elected to divert to Switzerland with his severely damaged plane. It was *Lillian Ann II's* 56th mission.

The work of the ground crews of any B-24 base was never done. If it didn't need repairing, then it needed regular maintenance, or it needed checking. Either way there was always plenty of work to get on with. Here the starboard, inner, Pratt & Whitney engine of one of the 445th's Liberators receives the full attention of these mechanics of its ground crew. This work went on, usually in the open on the hardstands, round the clock, regardless of the weather.

453rd Bomb Group – Old Buckenham

On Tuesday 30 May '44 on returning from a mission to bomb the Luftwaffe airfield at Oldenburg, south of Wilhelmshaven, 1st Lt. Wilbur Earl's luck ran out and *Golden Gaboon* crashed and burned on landing at Old Buckenham.

(Above) *Zeus*, (42-95353) of the 735th Bomb Squadron, another B-24 H out of the Ford Motor Company plant at Willow Run, also came to grief following the Oldenburg mission. It was flown that day by the Baer crew. The starboard outer engine was already feathered, prior to the landing and it is assumed that the damage to both port engines occurred after touchdown as it slithered off the runway on to the grass.

(Opposite page) WWII folklore has it that the Boeing B-17 could take a lot of damage and make it home. *Queenie*, this B-24 H (41-28631) proved that the Consolidated design could do the same. On Thursday 20 April '44, this Liberator of the 735th Bomb Squadron from the 453rd Bomb Group at Old Buckenham had the rear turret, tail plane and rudders virtually obliterated by flak during a mission to hit one of the German V-weapons installations on the French coast. The ground crew later counted more than 200 flak holes in the fuselage between the front and rear gun turrets.

Borsuk's Bitch a B-24 H (42-64496) of the 735th Bomb Squadron was damaged by flak on the 25 April '44 during the raid on the Mannheim Railway Marshalling Yards. Pilot, 1st Lt. Louis Scharzer, executed a successful forced landing at Dubendorf Airfield in Switzerland. The USAAF insignia and group markings were later painted out of this Fort Worth built bomber and the plane was repaired and test flown by the Swiss Air Force.

Whiskey Jingles of the 733rd Bomb Squadron, was an H model B-24, (42-51114).
The nose art on this Douglas Aircraft Company, Tulsa built, Liberator was just minimalist lettering in bright red. To further aid identification at the 453rd Bomb Group, the propeller spinners of the squadrons aircraft were all painted with different colours. The 733rd were blue, those of the 732nd were white, the 734th red and the 735th yellow.

Liberty Run, christened at a Christmas Eve party thrown by the 453rd Bomb Group at Old Buckenham for some of the local children. *Liberty Run* (42-110078) was a B-24 J out of the Consolidated's San Diego factory. It sported some of the largest nose art in the group and possibly the whole of the 2nd Air Division.

Spare Parts, a B-24 H (41-28654) of the 732nd Bomb Squadron heading back to Norfolk from its mission to bomb Achmer Airfield on Monday, 21 Feb 1944. As part of the operation known as 'Big Week', the USAAF's 8th Air Force also hit the airfields at Gutersloh, Lippstadt, Werl, Hopsten, Rheine, Diepholz, Quakenbruck and Bramsche on the same day. The majority of the contrails above *Spare Parts* are from the fighter escorts, shepherding their charges home. Just a few weeks later, *Spare Parts* was badly damaged during the Berlin raid 6 May 1944.

A small selection of the 453rd Bomb Group's nose art. As with all USAAF 8th Air Force Bomb groups, the subject matter at the 453rd was wide and varied, but as always, centred mainly on humour and glamour.

14th Bombardment Wing

44th Bomb Group – Shipdham

Shortly after their arrival at Shipdham in late 1942, B-24 D's from the 66th, 67th and 68th squadrons of the 44th Bomb Group, taxi out, past acres of mud, to start a practice mission and to familiarise themselves with their local area. (41-23818) *Miss Marcia Ann*, had arrived on 20 Sept. On Wednesday 16 Feb '43, during the raid on the airfield at St Nazaire; it collided with another B-24, caught fire and exploded. The wreckage fell through a squadron of B17s flying below them and into the sea near Selsey Bill, off the Sussex coast.

  (41-24225) the infamous 68th Squadron Liberator, *Flak Alley*, seen here flying low over Wymondham, just eight miles (4-5 flying minutes) south west of Shipdham airfield. In August it successfully took part in the legendry Ploesti mission, only to be lost over Gotha.

Even in 1943, if you got it wrong, there was a film crew there to record your exploits for posterity. Returning, severely damaged from a raid on Oslo-Kjeller, on 18 Nov, Lt. Rockford Griffith ordered his crew to bale out over Shipdham. Then with just one severely injured crew member left on board, he and his co-pilot Lt. Grono, successfully brought (41-29161) in on one wheel and three engines. It was a pretty wild ride.

This whole incident was captured on (amateur?) B/W footage, that still exists today. Not surprisingly Lt. Griffith was awarded the Silver Star for his efforts. 161 was an H model, built by Consolidated at their Fort Worth, Texas, plant. It had arrived on 9 Oct and was flown that same day by a crew borrowed from the 579th Bomb Squadron of the 392nd Bomb Group at Wendling.

J model B-24 (42-100330) built by Consolidated in San Diego, was delivered just before the end of January 1944. By late March that year it had already been in to Manston to have #4 engine replaced. Little wonder that the pilot, Lt. Rockford Griffith (the very same), elected to divert in to Switzerland when even more mechanical failures started to beset it, on 13 April. That was just four days after it had been released to service and flown back to Shipdham for use in a raid on the fighter assembly plant at Lechfield.

There is no record of the plane ever being named, despite the majestic 'flying blonde' artwork. There are no records of Lt. Griffith's comments either.

These shots were taken in the early morning of Thursday 12 April 1945. The war was drawing to a close, but a careful, thorough pre-flight check was still needed by the ground crews, just as it had been at the start of the USAAF's war in late '42 when the 44th Bomb Group first moved into Shipdham. Here the construction of the roller system of the bomb-bay doors is clearly evident on this B-24.

With bomb bay doors partially opened and a full load of bombs waiting to be loaded, for this B-24 it looked like just another day in the push to defeat the enemy. Today however it was not to be and the 44th Bomb Group's mission to Tirstrup in Mid April '45 was aborted. Two days later they attacked the German troop positions in Fort-De-Royen, France.

High over Hamburg, the 44th at work. In the foreground is the J model B-24, *My Gal Sal*, flown by Lt. Bentcliffe and his crew from the 506th Bomb Squadron. *My Gal Sal* (42-50626), was a Ford built aircraft out of Willow Run. It was written off for spares following a landing accident during which its nose wheel collapsed, on Wednesday 30 August 1944. It had only been delivered to the 44th on 1 July that year. The collapse or malfunction of the B-24 nose wheel was one of the more common mechanical failures of the Consolidated design.

Classic USAAF Liberator shots. Part of the formation of the 68th Squadron, en-route to Saarbrucken during the spring of '44, seen from the waist gunner's position. *Puritanical Bitch* , (42-50427) a B-24 H out of Fort Worth is nearest the camera.

    Lady Geraldine, (44-10504) one of 68th Squadron's J models, again seen through the waist gunner's window. It returned to the USA (ZOI) at the war's end on Thursday 31 May 1945.

Rugged Buggy of the 68th Bomb Squadron, lost with the James O'Brien crew on the Kiel mission on Friday 14 May 1943. Its loss followed flak damage over the Friesian Islands en-route to the target and repeated attacks by Me109s and FW 190 fighters on the way home. (41-23819) was one of the ten original B-24 Ds that arrived with the 44th Bomb Group in the autumn of the previous year.

Victory Ship, (41-23813) a D model of 68th Squadron, gets pulled out of the 464th Sub-depot hangar on the Tech Site at Shipdham. No doubt its repairs are complete and it is ready for its next mission. 813 first flew with the 44th in Sept '42. It flew the Ploesti mission, and diverted into Malta.

Repairs were always quick, though sometimes never finished off completely. Here (41-23811), 'K', a D model out of San Diego also sometime named *Fascinating Witch,* taxis out for a mission with the repairs to its starboard rear fin still un-painted. It also flew in the Ploesti raid on 1 August '43, and was lost in October the same year on the Wiener – Neustadt raid.

392nd Bomb Group – Wendling

B-24s of the 392nd Bomb Group from Wendling, en route to attack the legendry Bielefeld Railway Viaduct on 10 March '45, just as the war was drawing to a close.

The Liberator closest to the camera is *El Capitan*, an H model (41-28772), built by the Douglas Aircraft Company at their Tulsa Oklahoma plant. As can be seen from the state of the nose art, it was a much travelled, well used aircraft. It was originally assigned to the 44th Bomb Group at Shipdham, before being passed on the 491st at North Pickenham, and eventually making its way to Wendling and the 392nd in late '44.

Other times the nose art was fine, but the aircraft was not in such good shape. Here *El Lobo* of the 579th Bomb Squadron at Wendling was hit by flying debris (believed to be a complete propeller assembly) from another B-24 in the same formation on the raid on Bremen on Thursday 20 Dec 1943. It was a return visit, the 392nd having been to Bremen just 4 days earlier. Amazingly *El Lobo*, an H model (42-7510), flew over 500 miles in this condition.

Late on in its career, *Ford's Folly* being loaded by the 392nd's armourers with fragmentation cluster bombs, in preparation for the 6 June, D-day, raids. The 14th Bomb Wing flew three missions to support the landings, that day, to Collesville/St Laurent, Ferets-De-Cersy and Caen (Vire). It is possible *Ford's Folly* flew on all three. Certainly several of the 14th Bomb Wing's B-24's did. Note the recently added observation blister in front of the logo 'Ford's Folly', and the very impressive mission tally. This will be mission thirty-six.

Poop Deck Pappy, a Ford Motor Company built H model (42-7521) originally flew from Wendling, but never completed any combat missions with the 392nd Bomb Group, before being transferred to the 44th at Shipdham. It was severely damaged in a crash landing on the return from the 26 November '43 mission to Bremen. After repairs taking almost two months, it was then transferred to the 448th Bomb Group at Seething.

The puffs of rubber tyre smoke mark the touchdown point for *Pregnant Peg* (42-7491) arriving back at Wendling. 491 was an H model flown by the 577th Bomb Squadron.

On transferring to the 3rd SAD at Watton for repairs, the nose oleo collapsed, damaging the underside and rippling the aircraft outer skin behind the nose turret. The extensive repair work needed to put '491' back in the air was carried out by the heavy repair team at the Griston site at Watton. It was later lost on the Oranienburg mission on 3 March '44.

The 44th BG at Shipdham also had their own *Pregnant Peg*, (42-50328).

Two superb airborne shots of B-24 H (42-50433) of the 578th Bomb Squadron from the 392nd Bomb Group at Wendling. 433 was another Willow Run B-24.

Queen of Peace, a B-24 H, (42-7637) of the 577th Bomb Squadron, being dismantled at Smedstorp in Sweden by personnel of the Swedish Air Force. Its pilot, Lt. L. Page, was forced to divert and crash land 637 following the Kiel raid on 4 Jan '44. 637 was from the first batch of H models from The Ford Motor Company.

The crew and passengers (almost certainly all the plane's own ground crew) of Liberator *Monotonous Maggie* are briefed just before take-off. On this flight, instead of heading south and east, their track will turn north then west, as its pilot Lt. Steck and his flight crew, take the B-24 H (42-95151) and its personnel home to America, at the war's end. 151 originated at the Ford Motor Company plant at Willow Run.

491st/492nd Bomb Groups – North Pickenham

Although wearing incorrect squadron markings, (3X should read 6X), this H model B-24 (42-95218) from North Pickenham would later come to grief with a fire in No 2 engine.

Its pilot, 2/Lt. Stanley V. Scott, elected to divert to Dubendorf during the bombing mission to the Kempen Marshalling Yards on Friday 21 July 1944. By then the correct markings had been applied.

Nose Art . . . 491st style.

Flying Jackass a J model (44-40239) of 853rd Squadron. The nose art had nine chaps sitting on the donkey on the starboard side, eight on the port. Hopefully the guy painting the bomb on (44-40122) may not be the one who miscounted on the *Flying Jackass*.

While *House of Rumor* (44-40271) was probably one of the more detailed pieces.

Here's to You has to have one of the most prestigious mission records for the 14th Bomb Wing. There are 88 missions to its credit - so far.

1 October 1944, *Bi-U-Baby*, B-24 H (42-95619) an ex 44th Bomb Group aircraft, from the 855th BS of the 491st Bomb Group prepares to take off from Lydd Beach in Kent. On Friday 8 September following a raid on the Karlsruhe Marshalling Yards, while operating in a PFF role, its crew was forced to put it down on Lydd's expansive shingle beach. Once repairs had been carried out, a temporary runway was prepared and *Bi-U-Baby* was flown back to North Pickenham.

Sunday 15 April, 1945, the war has only days left to run. Napalm canisters follow a smoke marker from the bomb bay of this J model B-24 of the 854th Bomb Squadron (42-51493) over Fort-De-Royan, France, aimed at embattled German troop concentrations below. The smoke canister and the extended radome indicate this 491st Liberator was flying in a pathfinder (PFF) role that day.

B-24 J (42-50668) of the 854th Bomb Squadron, passing low over the Group's technical site at North Pickenham, in training for a low-level supply drop. It had completed twenty-six missions. It met its end at 16.25 on Monday 19 Feb.'45 on Black Hemaldon Moor near Burnley, Lancashire, during a ferry flight for maintenance at Burtonwood. Sadly eight out of the enlarged crew of eleven on board that day (five aircrew and six passengers), perished in the crash. The pilot was Lt. Charles A. Goeking. He was thrown through the windscreen and survived, 668 was an ex 44th Bomb Group aircraft, transferred to the 491st on 18 August '44, although it had not flown operationally with the 44th.

Posing beside 'their' Bomber was a rite of passage of every crew in the USAAF, not just the 2nd Air Division. Here the crew of *Rage in Heaven*, adopt the required pose beside their B-24 J (44-40165) of 852nd Bomb Squadron. *Rage in Heaven* was later declared War Weary and became the 491st's second assembly ship.

Lt. Alfred Mousette and his crew with *The Moose*, their B-24 J, (44-40205). They flew with the 853rd Bomb Squadron.

The crew of *Green Hornet*, a 852nd Squadron B-24 J (44-20468). 468 was an ex 492nd Bomb Group aircraft.

20th Bombardment Wing

93rd Bomb Group – Hardwick

Hellsadroppin'II, (41-23809) a B-24 D of the 329th Bomb Squadron of the 93rd Bombardment Group returns safely to its home base of Hardwick, south of Norwich.

809 was built by The Consolidated Aircraft Corporation at their San Diego factory as a part of Contract DA-4. 809 was later transferred to the 448th to become their assembly ship, *You Cawn't Miss It*.

B-24 Ds from the 93rd Bomb Group practise their low-level formation flying over Norfolk, prior to shipping out to Africa for the legendry mission against the Romanian Oil Fields at Ploesti in August 1943. The Liberators nearest camera on the bottom photo are (41-23990) *Heinie Hunter* and (41-23711) *Jerks Natural*, both San Diego built by Consolidated.

A classic B-24 Liberator shot. In clear sky, high above enemy territory, this 93rd Bomb Group B-24 was photographed by another bomber in the squadron formation, flying just a few hundred feet above it.

If one of the 2nd AD B-24s was too badly damaged to be repaired at its home airfield it would be diverted in to the 3rd SAD at Watton (Griston) for repair or salvage. Occasionally the plane was too badly damaged to make a successful landing and this sort of 'arrival' was the result. Seen here in November '43, (42-63974) a B-24 D of the 409th Bomb Squadron of the 93rd BG, slides off the runway with the port undercarriage collapsed and the port outer propeller ripped off. Amazingly the port inner propeller appears to have only minor damage to one blade.

Jerk's Natural, B-24 D (41-23711), another of the earlier Consolidated, San Diego built Liberators from the DA-4 Contract. 711 was another 2nd AD aircraft that took part in the Ploesti raid.

One of the war's earliest causalities, for the USAAF's 2nd AD. The end of *Katy Bug*.

(41-23745), a B-24 D built at the San Diego plant of The Consolidated Aircraft Corporation as part of Contract DA-4. 745 crashed at Alconbury (its temporary base) on return from the Lorient raid on the Brest Peninsula on Wednesday 18 Nov 1942.

The ordnance crews of the 93rd Bomb Group hard at work prior to another mission for the 2nd AD. Here the 1,000 lb bombs are fitted with fins and fuses before being loaded aboard the B-24 *Eager Beaver* (41-23737) ready for the trip to mainland Europe.

Exterminator, a B-24 D (41-23717). Built by The Consolidated Aircraft Corporation at their San Diego plant, it was flown by the 329th Bomb Squadron., of the 93rd.

The crew of 1st Lt. Hugh R. Roper photographed just before setting off in *Exterminator* on another mission.

A perfect landing from a B-24 of the 93rd as demonstrated above, was not always possible.

Flak damage on (42-110072), a B-24 J of the 330th Bomb Squadron, prevented its pilot from pulling off a text book landing. 072 was returning from a raid on Coulommiers Airfield in France, on Friday 11 August '44.

B-24 M (44-50579) of the 328th Bomb Squadron, 93rd Bomb Group, in formation high over the Alps with an unidentified B-24 L of the 329th Bomb Squadron. Earlier D models from the 93rd, low over the Mediterranean Sea during one of their North African detachments.

93rd Bomb Group Nose Art.

Satan's Angels, a B-24 D out of San Diego. (42-40604)

Celhalopdos, another San Diego D model (41-23675) built almost a year earlier by Consolidated.

The Urgin' Virgin, (42-41004) of the 329th Bomb Squadron undergoing repairs at the 3rd SAD at Watton, Sep 1943. 004 was a J model out of Fort Worth.

Solid Comfort, (42-50501), seen here close to the war's end in March 1945. 501 was an H model from the Consolidated, Fort Worth plant. 501 flew with the 330th Bomb Squadron.

446th Bomb Group – Bungay (Flixton)

An early shot of the 446th Bombardment Group at work. Here (42-100360) *Luck and Stuff* a B-24 J of the 706th Bomb Squadron at Bungay, formates with other Squadron B-24s on their way to today's target. On this mission it was an aircraft assembly plant at Gotha, some 40 miles south-west of Kassel in Germany *Luck and Stuff* was Consolidated built B-24 out of San Diego.

Wednesday Morning, 24 May 1944 and Orly Airport in the southern outskirts of Paris takes a pounding from the 446th Bomb Group. Here a B-24 of the 704th Bomb Squadron adds to the devastation, thousands of feet below. Many French airfields received the same attention from the 2nd AD during May and June of that year.

14 June '44, another enemy held airfield takes a pounding from the 446th Bomb Group. This time it was Orleans-Briey Airfield that was the immediate focus of attention for the B-24s of the 706th Bomb Squadron. Here (42-50318) one the Consolidated built B-24 H out of Fort Worth, unloads over target. The yellow bomb door position indicator lines on 318 can be clearly seen.

Red Ass, a Ford Built B-24 H (42-95203) of the 704th Bomb Squadron at Flixton, high above Germany on Friday morning 10 November 1944 on the mission to bomb the airfield at Hanau. Earlier in June '44 it was believed that 203 was the first 8th Air Force plane over the D-Day invasion beaches. In March '45, 203 sustained this flak damage to its rear rudder assembly on a low-level raid to support the Rhine crossings. Finally repaired, it went back to the USA at the war's end; stopping here at Goose Bay, Labrador on the ferry flight home.

Desperate Desmond, a B-24 H (42-7498) of the 706th Bomb Squadron, in formation with the 446th, Bomb Group, en-route to Frankfurt, Friday 11 February 1944. 498 was one of the first B-24 H models out of the Ford Motor Company plant at Willow Run. It was salvaged as War Weary in May 1945.

Wolf Patrol, (42-50882) one of the 705th Bomb Squadron's B-24 Js unloading over Salzburg Marshalling Yards on Wednesday 25 April 1945. It was the 446th's final ETO mission.

A year or more earlier *Lazy Lou,* (42-7609) *Old Faithful* (42-7505) and *The Spirit of 77* (42-6707) all H models head out over Europe to take their turn to inflict damage on the enemy.

The 446th in formation, high over English countryside lead by B-24 J (42-50814) and other aircraft from the 706th Bomb Squadron. 814 was a Ford built Liberator from Contract 21216, which ordered a total of over six thousand B-24s of various models from the Ford Motor Company.

Patriotic Patty, a B-24 J (42-50734) out of the Ford plant at Willow Run. 734 was flown by the 707th Bomb Squadron of the 446th. Top picture it is on the perimeter track at Bungay, displaying an impressive mission tally. (75 to date.) In the bottom picture 734 is high over Germany, en-route to a low-level supply drop to allied ground troops along the river Rhine. The date is 24 March 1945 and the war has only a few weeks to run.

Things did not always go well for the 446th. Here *Merle Lee*, (42-7584) a B-24 H from the 706th Bomb Squadron, originally built at Willow Run, is seen here being dismantled at Hawkinge in Kent. 584 crash landed on returning from a raid on the V-weapons site near Cherbourg on Friday 21 January 1944.

A few weeks later, on Thursday 8 March 1944, the shattered remains of the tails section of *Shift'lus Skunk*, a B-24 H (42-7595) of the 706th Bomb Squadron lay scattered in a wood on the outskirts of Berlin.

448th Bomb Group – Seething

The 448th practise formation flying over Norfolk. This shot was taken shortly after the 448th's arrival at Seething. The B-24 H in the foreground is *Lady from Bristol* (42-52100), a Ford built Liberator out of Willow Run. 100 flew with the 714th Bomb Squadron and failed to return from the Amiens raid on 25 February 1944. It was its 14th mission.

A later formation of the 448th . . . this time for real. Overhead Frankfurt on Sunday 29 January 1944. (42-7764) in the foreground was a B-24 H built by Ford. It was from the first batch of H models built at the new Willow Run Plant. It was badly damaged during its thirteenth mission and ran off the end of the runway, with a fire in its right wing.

A second formation of the 714th Bomb Squadron from the 448th with *Peggy Jo* another B-24 H (42-94774) in the foreground, 774 was also a Ford built Liberator. It was a victim of the 22 April '44 intruder attack. It crashed in flames at Worlingham, near Beccles.

Wolf Pack, (42-52121) a B-24 H of the 713th Bomb Squadron, is rescued from the muddy wastes of Seething, following a nose oleo collapse during a crash landing on Friday 8 September 1944. *Wolf Pack* was a Ford built aircraft out of Willow Run, against the 11 April 1942 section of Order 21216.

Hello Natural II, (42-52606) a B-24 of the 712th Bomb Squadron of the 448th was involved in a catastrophic ground accident whilst wounded crewmen were being unloaded. On returning from the 2nd AD's second raid on Saarbrucken's rail and communication centre that week, on Sunday 16 July 1944, 606 was struck at the rear of the fuselage by another B-24 and the plane sheared in two just behind the waist gunner's positions.

Dead End Kids, a B-24 H (42-94992) of the 713th Bombardment Squadron, undergoing major repairs at the 3rd Strategic Air Depot (3rd SAD) at Watton. This Ford built Liberator was badly shot up in January 1945 and was forced to make an emergency landing in Belgium. It was made good and then flown back to the 3rd SAD for further work.

Fat Stuff II, a B-24 H (42-7591) from the 712th Bomb Squadron of the 448th at Seething, was one of the only batch of H models built by The Ford Motor Company at their Willow Run facility to Contract 21216. 591 is seen here returning from a raid on Berlin on Thursday 22 March 1944. It was one of the 2nd AD's first visits to the German capital . . . it would not be their last. 591 force landed in Switzerland following the 12 July raid on Munich. It was normal practice with B-24s, for one crew member to act as observer while the plane taxied to its hardstand.

A selection of Nose Art from the 448th Bomb Group.

Old 75, (42-50391) a B-24 M, flew with the 713th Bomb Squadron. It was Ford built aircraft out of the Willow Run, originally delivered to the 492nd Bomb Group.

The Rabduckit, (42-100435) the last of 900 aircraft built by Consolidated at their San Diego plant for Contract 35312. 435 flew with the 715th and the 714th Bomb Squadrons.

Leading Lady, (42-48805) from the 712th Bomb Squadron.

Miss America, (44-10554), a B-24 J from the 713th Bomb Group. 554 was a Consolidated built aircraft out of Fort Worth, Texas.

On afternoon of Saturday 22 April 1944, German fighters followed the 448th home following the raid on the Marshalling yards at Hamm, and shot up the returning B-24s as they descended towards the airfield and made their final approach to Seething. Seven aircraft were damaged, three severely, and two crews were lost.

Captain, (42-50388) a B-24 H of the 846th Bomb Squadron, sits next to a Boeing B17 Flying Fortress at RAF Woodbridge following the raid on Ehrang on Saturday 26 August 1944. This was *Captain's* 40th and final trip. RAF Woodbridge was an emergency airfield equipped with an enormous east / west runway that measured 3000 yards by 250 yards, with 500 yard grass extensions at either end. It was the main emergency diversion airfield for returning bombers from both the RAF and the USAAF.

Nose Art 489th style.

Cover Girl, a B-24 H (42-94945) flown by the Elliott crew of the 846th Bomb Squadron.

Pin Up Girl, (42-94941) another H model. It flew with the 846th Bomb Squadron until transferred to the 446th Bomb Group.

Struggle Buggy Another of the Ford built Willow Run built H models, (42-94785).

Plate's Date, an H model (42-94830) operated by the 847th Bomb Squadron. It crashed at Leiston on returning from the raid on Criel on 2 June 1944.

Tiger's Revenge of the 846th Bomb Squadron. (42-94816) was a B-24 H.

Struggle Bunny (42-94785) following the mission to bomb the Strasbourg fuel dumps on 11 August, '44. *Struggle Buggy's* pilot. Lt Maynard Kisinger elected to divert his B-24 H to Dubendorf in Switzerland, rather than risk the lives of his crew trying to get the flak damaged plane back to Halesworth.

The Legendary *Sharon D* of the 845th Bomb Squadron of the 489th Bomb Group overhead the burning Misburg oil plant. 12 September 1944. Col. Leon Vance standing beside the *Sharon D*, named after his young daughter (the real Sharon D), seen here in her father's arms. *Sharon D* (42-94759) was a B-24 H out of the Ford plant at Willow Run from Contract 21216. 759 was later transferred to the 445th Bomb Group.

Bomber's Moon, (42-94903) a B-24 H of the 844th Bomb Squadron high over Speyerdorf Airfield (between Kaiserslautern and Mannheim), Tuesday 3 October 1944. The smoke canisters indicate the airfield position just off photo. 2 weeks later 903 had a mid-air collision with (42-94913) and crashed over the target.

96th Bombardment Wing

458th Bomb Group – Horsham St Faith

B-24 H (41-28678) of the 458th Bomb Group, in a classic touch down pose at the end of the Horsham St Faith main runway. 678 was a Tulsa built Liberator from the 755th Bomb Squadron. It was lost on the Berlin mission on Wednesday 22 March 1944.

An accident while taxiing was enough to write off this B-24 H(41-29302) *Nokkish*. The accident occurred at Horsham St Faith on Thursday 29 April 1944 when the starboard main wheel of 301 ran off the perimeter track and into a small ditch.

Final Approach, a B-24 H (42-52457) leads the 752nd Bomb Squadron and other 458th Bomb Group Liberators around the eastern perimeter track to the threshold of Horsham's runway 23. It was to be the 458th's 200th mission, and Berlin was the target. There are at least 26 B-24s on this section of the perimeter-track. *Final Approach* had 122 missions to its credit when it was shot down on 9 April 1945, during the attack on Lechfield airfield. The war had just weeks to run.

Paddlefoot, a B24-H (41-28719) at the start of its operational career with just two indicators on its mission tally board. Some time later this stalwart of the 755th Bomb Squadron has amassed thirty-six missions and is still looking ready for more.

Whoever logged 716's mission tally had his own unique ideas on how to do it.

B-24 J *Bad Girl,* (44-40288) of the 753rd Bomb Squadron. Initially seen as it taxis away from its hard stand at Horsham St Faith. Later, on Monday 2 October, 1944 *Bad Girl* crash landed following a practise flight. 288 was built by Consolidated at the San Diego plant in California as part of contract 40033. It was part of a large single order run of B-24 J types of over 1300 aircraft.

Nose Art from the 458th.

Ole' Satan, B-24 H (41-29298)

Wolves Lair, B-24 H (41-29352)

Bombs Away, B-24 H (42-95096)

Sky Room, B-24 J (42-50578)

Nokkish, B-24 H (41-29302)

Meat Around The Corner, B-24 H (41-28738)

The Shack, A B-24 J (44-40298) of the 754th Bomb Squadron, seen preparing for take off for the Berlin raid on the morning of Monday 26 February 1945. While in England *The Shack's* delightful nose adornment went 'au natural'. By the time she returned to Willow Run in America at the cessation of hostilities, she had acquired some underwear! 298 had flown with the 487th and 493rd Bomb Groups, before the 3rd Air Division converted to the Boeing B17 Flying Fortress.

The Technical Site and its hangars was always the heart of any Bomb Group's maintenance and repair operation. B-24s and hangars went together. In the top picture *The Pied Piper*, a B-24 H (42-51206) of the 752nd Bomb Squadron stands ready to return to service. 206 was a Douglas Aircraft Company built aircraft, out of Tulsa, Oklahoma.

The autumn of 1944 saw an adventurous few weeks for *Gas House Mouse*, (42-95050) a B-24 H of the 752nd Bomb Squadron. 050 had to make a forced landing near the village of Framlingham, south of Norwich, on October 1944, then just a few weeks later while returning from the raid on Hanau on Monday 11 December, it was again forced to make an emergency landing, with the starboard inner engine feathered. This time it was at RAF Manston in Kent where these photos were taken.

466th Bomb Group – Attlebridge

Pegasus-The Flying Red Horse a B-24 H (42-51141) of the 748th Bomb Squadron relies on parachute braking after experiencing hydraulic failure. The chutes were attached to the gun mounts to take the loading. The 748th were part of the 466th Bomb Group based at Attlebridge, eight miles to the south of Norwich.

The thoughts of the 466th
Bomb Group on Nose Art.
  This Above All, a B-24 J
(44-40328)
  Damifino, a B-24 J
(42-50465)
  Jamaica? a B-24 H
(41-28746)
  AINT Miss Behavin' a B-24 H
(42-52509)
  Biff – Bam a B-24 H
(42-95283)

Fran (44-49582) a B-24 L Pathfinder (PFF), from the 785th Bomb Squadron of the 446th, leads other B-24s from the 785th Bomb Squadron to their target with it's H2X scanner radome lowered. 582 was a Ford built B-24 out of Willow Run. Only the Willow Run and San Diego plants built the L model.

(opposite page:) *Times A' Wastin'*, a B-24 J (42-50569) of the 785th Bomb Squadron suffered this unusual damage to its prop, from flak. 569 was on the mission to bomb 'targets of opportunity' in and around the Bremerhaven and Wesermunde areas at the mouth of the River Weser along the North Coast of Germany on Sunday 18 June 1944.

Lovely Lady's Avenger a B-24 J (44-40093), a San Diego built Liberator from the large 40033 Contract. *Lovely Lady's Avenger* flew with the 786th Bomb Squadron of the 466th Bomb Group. It came to grief following an emergency landing in Sweden on Wednesday 21 June 1944 following a raid on Berlin. It was flown that day by Lt. L. Mower and his crew.

The Falcon, a B-24 H (42-95248) of the 785th Bomb Squadron from Attlebridge crashed near Shipdham Airfield (Station 115), home of the 44th Bomb Group, on Monday 8 January 1945.

In the top photo, rescuers can be seen wading through knee high, freezing water of a pond to lift the casualty's stretchers away from the wreckage of *The Falcon*. 248 was built at the Ford Motor Company's Willow Run Factory as part of Contract 21216.

One of the early losses for the 466th Bomb Group. *Shack Date,* a B-24 H (42-52566) of the 786th Bomb Squadron came to grief at Attlebridge, when returning from the raid on Paderborn Airfield on Wednesday 19 April 1944. There was not much left to salvage.

B-24s of the 784th and 787th Bomb Squadrons go to work. High Explosive (HE) bombs follow the smoke canisters down to the enemy installations below. *Peck's Bad Boys*, B-24 J (42-51353), B-24 J (42-51531) and *Hard Luck* B-24 J (44-40253) lead the formation over the target.

Winter weather was no friend to the 2nd Air Division. Here a mixture of frost, snow and fog adds to the 466th's problems, in early 1945. B-24 J (42-51699) *Duffy's Tavern* sits in solitary isolation on its hardstand, awaiting better weather. *Laden Maid Again*, a B-24 J (44-10521), B-24 J (42-50503), and *Parsons Chariot* a B-24 M,(44-50699), of the 784th Bomb Squadron, all waiting for a change of conditions for the better.

B-24 (42-51198) fully ablaze following an electrical fault that got rapidly out of hand.

On Wednesday 8 November 1944, this Liberator was totally lost without any enemy involvement whatsoever. Here the 466th's fire crews fight a loosing battle at Hard Stand 45 to save anything from the blaze. It is interesting to note the complete lack of safety clothing and kit for the fire crews and the diminutive size of the appliances they were expected to use.

467th Bomb Group – Rackheath

Valiant Lady, a B-24 H (41-29408) of the 790th Bomb Squadron, low over the North Sea.

408 was a Consolidated Aircraft Corporation built aircraft out of their Fort Worth, Texas factory.

Angel, a B-24 H (42-95057) just seconds from touchdown at Station 145, Rackheath.

Angel flew with the 790th Bomb Squadron. 057 was built by the Ford Motor Company at the Willow Run factory as part of Contract 21216.

Stinger, a B-24 H (42-52542) seriously damaged following a landing accident at Watton. In the centre picture, field repairs are sufficient to enable it to be towed off the airfield to the hangars; however subsequent photos showed a great deal of damage requiring attention.

Detailed photos show the true extent of the damage to *Stinger*. Lt. Murphy and his crew, from the 791st Bomb Squadron were diverted to the 3rd SAD at Watton because of the severe damage the aircraft had sustained during the raid on Brunswick on Monday 8 May 1944.

467th Nose Art.
  Blonde Bomber. (42-50471)
  Pete the Pom Inspector 2nd. B-24 H (41-29393)
  Feudin Wagon. B-24 J (44-40155)
  Witchcraft. B-24 H (42-52534) of the 790th Bomb Squadron, a veteran of 130 missions.

Wallowing Wilbert, a B-24 H (41-29421) of the 791st Bomb Squadron at Rackheath gets a multiple engine change on its hardstand. The crew chief and his team would have their work cut out with a situation like this. *Wallowing Wilbert* was one of 493 B-24 Hs built at Fort Worth, Texas, against Contract 18723.

The crew of B-24 L (44-49610) from the 791st Bomb Squadron were pleased to walk away from this landing accident on 24 March 1945.

Whilst earlier in the post D-Day push through Europe, another 491st Bomb Squadron crew are equally pleased, but for other reasons, as they unloaded their collection of War Trophies.

Assembly Ships

Just imagine taking off from your airfield just before daybreak, climbing in half light to ten thousand feet, in the company of sixty or so other bombers? Then remember that at the same time, double that amount of B24s from the two other Bomb Groups in your wing are just a few miles from your own doing the same thing and heading more or less in the same direction. Your first task is for you all to meet up at some point in the sky above Norfolk . . . and not get in the way of several hundred other B24s from other Bomb Wings, all doing something similar, but from different directions.

If the weather is overcast, the instructions were to assemble 1,500ft above the cloud cover

Now I think you can see the necessity to have a garishly painted assembly ship to help you.

The brighter and more obvious the better!

The 389th BG at Hethel, painted up this 'War Weary' D model B24, formerly known as *Jo-Jo's Special Delivery*, (41-23683) and pressed it into service as the Group's Assembly ship. They renamed it *The Green Dragon*, after their local pub. On a regular basis between mid '44 and mid '45 it set off just ahead of the 389th's crews and loitered off the North Norfolk coast to shepherd its flock together before they all headed upwards with the rest of the 2nd Bombardment Wing Liberators and finally set off towards their targets in mainland Europe.

At Horsham St Faith, the 458th took recognition seriously. With a base airframe colour in white and the only other colours used being pink and purple, there was no way any of the boys would miss their assembly ship. Unlike most Liberators of the 2nd Air Division Bomb Groups, *The Spotted Ape* (41-28967) was a later H model, built at the Douglas Aircraft Company plant at Tulsa Oklahoma. Originally she had flown as *Dixie Belle 2nd*. A similar colour scheme had adorned the 458th's first assembly ship, a D model, *First Sergeant* (42-40127).

Ball of Fire, (41-23667) the Assembly Ship for the 93rd Bomb Group, seen here passing low over the village of Hempnall just to the north of its base at Hardwick. Its colours were bright red, white and light blue, The colours changed regular over the months.

Ball of Fire was one of the first B-24 Ds out of the Consolidated Aircra Corporation's plant in San Diego on Contract DA-4.

Over at Shipdham Airfield (Station 115) , the 44th Bomb Group took a slightly different view of conspicuity. Not so much the startling approach, rather the big and obvious. Large swathes of vertical yellow stripes, separated by much thinner black ones, made *Lemon Drop* (41-23699) stand out in even the murkiest East Anglian, winter morning. It would never be a contender for the most imaginative design, but it was certainly one of the most effective.

The scores under the cockpit show that it had already had a highly commendable career in bombing with the 68th Bomb Squadron, before being decorated and pressed into service as the 44th's assembly ship early in '44. The front turret shows clearly that the removal of armament was a common feature of most assembly ships. The 'Flying Eightball' group logo has been preserved despite the new paint job and can be clearly seen. The 44th were the only group to have their jacket patch transferred to all their operational aircraft.

Lemon Drop (41-23699) was a D variant of the B24, built at the Consolidated Aircraft Corporation plant in San Diego, California. Delivered to the 44th on 20 Sept '42, it flew the Ploesti mission in August '43. In April the following year it was 'retired' as war weary and assigned to assembly ship duties. It had two periods away from Shipdham during '44 for major repairs and was eventually ordered to the scrap yard, after the War's end, on 1st June 1945 having failed its POM (Prior to Overseas Movement) inspection.

No one could accuse the 392nd at Wendling of copying the simple but obvious approach of the boys of the 44th. This D model Liberator (41-23689), originally named *Minerva*, carried what was almost certainly the most complex paint scheme of any 2nd Air Division assembly ship. As well as it's duties as the Group's assembly ship, in April 1945 it was also used for experimental work on the feasibility of the troop carrying capability of a Liberator, believed to be assessing its ability to repatriate combat troops and personnel to the USA, after the war's end.

Assembly ships were also filled with marker lights using distinctive colours and patterns, These were housed in the rear gun turrets. Early morning fog, cloud, ice, and a low sun rising above cloud tops, all added to the crew's difficulty in identifying their own circling Group. Any assistance was always very welcome.

Like their buddies at the 44th, when it came to decorating 'their' assembly ships, the crews at the 448th at Seething, skipped the subtle approach and went straight for the big and bold. Previously *2nd Avenue El* (41-29489) was in maroon and white diagonals and *You Cawn't Miss It* (41-23809) previously *Hellsadroppin II* went for the chequerboard effect. As there is very little in nature that is visually straight, square or chequered, finding the 448th was never going to be a particularly hard task.

The tail light system on 8th Air Force Assembly Ships. Fitted locally, these light assembly units were easily to install and greatly assisted the effectiveness of the assembly ship procedures.

Sadly . . .

Sadly, one of the cruel facts of war is that not all aircraft that set off on a mission are always going to get home in one piece. Sometimes even the undoubted skill and bravery of the young B-24 pilots and their crews was not enough to keep their aircraft in the air any longer, or enable them to make a successful landing, even if they made it back to base. Although it has to be said, that a landing that the crew survived, was often considered a pretty good outcome, particularly when the wreckage was examined once it had come to rest.

If the plane had been damaged during the mission, then to get it back to England was the first priority; to get it to an airfield was the second. If it was your own airfield, then so much the better; you knew the emergency crews would be there for you.

Although several crash pictures feature in the previous pages, these were deemed worthy of inclusion.

Here the Lt. Conrad Menzel crew of one of the 44th Bomb Group's B-24Hs (42-50328) of the 506th BS return to the aircraft salvage some personal kit through the top escape hatch.

If wrecking the aircraft on landing after the mission like the Menzel crew, was unfortunate enough, you have to remember that it was not always essential to fly across Europe for misfortune to befall a B-24.

Some Liberators never made it off the ground on take off. Lt. Davidio did the best he could when his 44th B.G., B-24 H (41-29638) lost an engine on the take off run. It was 23 March 1944 and the mission was to have been to Osnabruck. Regardless of the when and why things went badly wrong, the end result to each aircraft was much the same.

All too often when the damage to the aircraft was too severe there was only ever going to be one outcome. Just a few hours earlier, this mass of tangled wreckage in a European wood, had been a fully serviceable B-24 of the 448th Bomb Group, taxiing along the perimeter track of their home base at Seething. When it all went terribly wrong, ten young men had been asked to pay the ultimate price.

Fire was always any aircrew's nightmare. Both of these B-24s from the 389th and 492nd Bomb Groups suffered a fire but with vastly differing outcomes. The engine fire on one was contained, but the fire that ripped through the other crashed Liberator destroyed almost everything in its path until the last of the plane's fuel ran out. German schoolchildren stare at the remains of B-24 J (44-40132).

When this B-24 from the 448th Bomb Group eventually came to rest it was dirty and damaged. The groove ploughed by the port wheel and undercarriage, before it collapsed, can be clearly seen in the foreground.

In the lower picture at another crash site, the injured aircrew are now in safe hands as they get lifted out of the aircraft through the waist gunner's window and sent on their way to hospital.

Final Approach, a B-24 H (42-52457) from the 752nd Bomb Squadron, 458th Bomb Group at Horsham St Faith, with its port fuel tank ruptured and ablaze, with only a few seconds left before it plunges to earth over Lechfeld, Monday 9 April 1945. It was *Final Approach's* 113th mission.

The War is over. Parked up outside the Ford Motor Company plant at Willow Run, Michigan in June '45, B-24s of the 392nd Bomb Group await their fate. They are (42-50650), (42-51194) *My Prayer*, (42-95250) and the 577th Bomb Squadron's (42-95040) *Silver Streak*.

For those that survived it was still not good. This was the ignominious fate that awaited the vast majority of all B-24s returning home after the War's end. Here row upon row of perfectly serviceable Liberators await the scrap man's cutters.

Amazingly just a few weeks earlier, after the peace documents were signed in Europe, dozens of crew chiefs across Norfolk were told they had to fit all the latest factory updates to their charges before they were allowed to fly with their aircrews, back to the United States. Occasionally when they returned home, they flew to an air base where dispersal of the crews and the 'civilianisation' of aircrew and ground crew alike, could commence. On other occasions they flew directly to a facility where the scrapping of these aircraft could commence. This scene was repeated time and time again across America in the summer of 1945 as thousands of redundant bombers came home.

Certainly the men were glad to be home, but on reflection this hardly seemed a fitting end for such faithful wartime stalwarts.

Ginny Gal (42-95077) flown by the Lt. Kay R. Caldwell crew from the 389th at Hethel, sustained flak damage and turned to the Swiss airfield at Dubendorf for an emergency landing. The port outer propeller appears to have been feathered prior to the landing. It was Friday 21 July 1944. The target that day had been the Railway Marshalling Yards at Saarbrucken. The Ford Built B-24 H was from the 565th Bomb Squadron.

Some accidents were more 'routine' than others. A nose wheel collapse as with this B-24 J (42-100343) at Tibenham was not unusual. 343 had been built at the Consolidated plant in San Diego. However when Lt. Watson of the 703rd Bomb Squadron from the 445th BG, crash landed *Kelly* at Manston, the final yards of the mission must have been pretty focusing for the crew, as well as the occupants of the hut.

BIBLIOGRAPHY

Consolidated B-24 Liberator, Edward Shacklady, Cerebus 2002

The 44th Bomb Group in Norfolk, Peter Bodle & Steve Adams, Liberator 2006

The 389th Bomb Group in Norfolk, Peter Bodle & Paul Wilson, Liberator 2006

The 492nd/491st Bomb Groups in Norfolk, Peter Bodle, Liberator 2006

The 458th Bomb Group in Norfolk, Peter Bodle & Mike Bailey, Liberator 2007

The 3rd SAD/ 25th Bomb Group in Norfolk, Peter Bodle & Ken Godfrey, Liberator 2007

The 392nd Bomb Group in Norfolk, Peter Bodle & John Gilbert, Liberator 2007

The 448th Bomb group in Norfolk, Peter Bodle & Patricia Everson, Liberator 2008

The Sky Scorpions, Paul Wilson & Ron Mackay, Schiffer 2006

The 44th Bomb Group in WWII, Steve Adams & Ron Mackay, Schiffer 2006

B-24 Liberator Groups, Mike Bailey, Red Kite 2007